Coping™

COPING WITH

ECOANXIETY

Marcia Amidon Lusted

Rosen
YA™

New York

*To all the young people who are working hard to
save both the planet and their futures.*

Published in 2020 by The Rosen Publishing Group, Inc.
29 East 21st Street, New York, NY 10010

Library of Congress Cataloging-in-Publication Data

Names: Lusted, Marcia Amidon, author.
Title: Coping with ecoanxiety / Marcia Amidon Lusted.
Description: First edition. | New York : Rosen Publishing, 2020. | Series: Coping |
Includes bibliographical references and index.
Identifiers: LCCN 2019009329| ISBN 9781725341173 (library bound) |
ISBN 9781725341166 (pbk.)
Subjects: LCSH: Environmental psychology—Juvenile literature. | Climatic changes—
Psychological aspects—Juvenile literature.
Classification: LCC BF353.5.C55 L87 2020 | DDC 155.9/15—dc23
LC record available at https://lccn.loc.gov/2019009329

Manufactured in China

On the cover: It seems like every day the media reports more bad news about climate
change. The ecoanxiety this causes is becoming more common and severe.

Some of the images in this book illustrate individuals who are models. The depictions
do not imply actual situations or events.

CONTENTS

INTRODUCTION

On October 29, 2012, Hurricane Sandy swept onto the northeastern coast of the United States. Its winds reached 80 miles per hour (128.7 kilometers per hour), classifying it as a Category 1 storm. Sandy's storm surge devastated coastal states, stretching from Florida to Maine. New Jersey, New York, and Connecticut were among those states most affected. Residents were trapped in flooded homes and had to be rescued to survive. Infrastructures were at the mercy of the dangerous hurricane. In New York City, the storm surge flooded subway tunnels, low-lying streets, and electrical systems. Skyscrapers swayed in the high winds, and a ship ran aground on Staten Island. As a result of Sandy's destructive force, 117 Americans died and 200,000 homes were damaged. Not only was Sandy one of the most expensive storms in US history, but it also contributed to a pattern of increasingly dangerous storms brought about by climate change.

According to Molly S. Castelloe's article on PsychologyToday.com, the International Psychoanalytical Association (IPA) labeled climate change as "the biggest global health threat of the 21st century." As the world experiences the results of this threat, many people realized how vulnerable they could be to changing climate

In 2012, the Brooklyn–Battery Tunnel in New York City was flooded from a tidal surge caused by Hurricane Sandy. Other parts of the city were overcome with floodwaters and debris.

conditions. These concerns, if they become more frequent, can lead to a form of anxiety known as ecoanxiety. In general, anxiety is the prolonged fear that something bad is or will happen. Ecoanxiety is the chronic fear that ongoing human development and pollution will cause global catastrophes, such as floods, heat waves, extreme weather patterns, species extinction, famines, and human migration. Results from these catastrophes could cause communities to suffer, unable to live safely, grow food, and raise the next generation. Those with ecoanxiety believe that climate change will lead to the final destruction of mankind. These thoughts, feelings, and beliefs manifest themselves in a long list of mental and physical reactions. Symptoms are unique to each individual. They can include physical pain, irritability, panic attacks, loss of appetite, insomnia (also known as habitual sleeplessness), nightmares, unexplained weakness, and depression. Triggers, which are reminders of a past trauma, can cause those with ecoanxiety to weep or grow angry when faced with negative news regarding negative effects on the environment. Examples include the extinction of a species or the melting of the polar ice caps. Sufferers could also feel hopeless, thinking their efforts are too minimal to turn things around for the better.

As natural disasters increase in number and severity, so do the cases of ecoanxiety for the world's population. Mental health care professionals are devoting research and resources to better understand this condition. Individuals of all ages are also learning how to recognize and cope with ecoanxiety. They reach out to community members, policymakers, and influential organizations to join them in taking steps to take action beyond the fear and build a better future for our planet.

CHAPTER ONE

A Warming World

According to UNFCCC.int, the Paris Climate Agreement of 2016 called upon all nations "to combat climate change and to accelerate and intensify the actions and investments needed for a sustainable low carbon future." World leaders from the 55 countries that were responsible for 55 percent of the world's carbon emissions signed the agreement, and it has since been ratified by 129 additional countries. The agreement's goal, as noted by UNFCCC.int, was to:

> ... strengthen the global response to the threat of climate change by keeping a global temperature rise this century well below 2 degrees Celsius [3.6 degrees Fahrenheit] above pre-industrial levels and to pursue efforts to limit the temperature increase even further to 1.5 degrees Celsius [2.7°F].

On April 22, 2016, actor and climate activist Leonardo DiCaprio spoke at the United Nations signing ceremony for the Paris Agreement.

Additionally, the agreement aims to strengthen the "ability of countries to deal with the impacts of climate change."

It is important to note the difference between the Celsius temperature scale, a part of the metric system that is used by the majority of the world's nations, and the Fahrenheit temperature scale that is used in the United States and a handful of other nations. Both measure temperature but require conversion for comparison. To convert Celsius to Fahrenheit, multiply the temperature by 1.8 (or 9/5) and add 32. Boiling water (at normal pressure) measures 100°C and 212°F. As it freezes, the water measures 0°C and 32°F.

After the Paris Agreement, the United Nations Framework Convention on Climate Change (UNFCCC) turned to the Intergovernmental Panel on Climate Change (IPCC) to assess the science related to climate change. The UNFCCC commissioned the IPCC to draft an important report known as the "Global Warming of 1.5°C." The 2018 report addressed the consequences of a warming planet, stating that the effects of human behavior were very real and very visible. The report urged communities around the world to take drastic measures to limit increasing temperatures. While most countries agreed in 2016 to limit global warming to just 2°C above the planet's temperature in the days before the Industrial Age, which began in the eighteenth century and ended in 1840, the report insisted that global warming be limited to an even smaller increase of just 1.5°C. Written in scientific language, the report stated that limiting global warming to 1.5°C would require "rapid, far-reaching and unprecedented changes in all aspects of society," as noted on IPCC.ch. According to ScienceDaily.com, Panmao Zhai, part of the IPCC group that helped write the report, said, "One of the key messages that comes out very strongly from this report is that we are already seeing the consequences of 1°C of global warming through more extreme weather, rising sea levels and diminishing Arctic sea

Pollution rises into a smog-filled sky from the smokestacks of the Jones and Laughlin steel mills in Pittsburgh, Pennsylvania, circa 1900.

ice, among other changes." The report made it clear that limiting global warming to 1.5°C, instead of 2°C as previously attempted, would make a tremendous difference. "Every extra bit of warming matters, especially since warming of 1.5°C or higher increases the risk associated with long-lasting or irreversible changes, such as the loss of some ecosystems," said Hans-Otto Pörtner, another IPCC scientist, as noted by ScienceDaily.com.

The Point of No Return

As soon as the "Global Warming of 1.5ºC" report was published, the news media began publishing headlines about the twelve years left to limit the climate change catastrophe. The world's population looked to 2030 as the point of no return for the survival of the planet. This was especially true if drastic measures were not taken to reduce carbon and greenhouse gas emissions, and attempts weren't made to immediately repair the damage that had been already been done. Other climate organizations agreed with the report, including the National Resource Defense Council (NRDC). According to NRDC.org, "A half degree more of warming would mean substantially more poverty, extreme heat, sea level rise, habitat loss, and drought. And we cannot prevent this unless we

The Big Difference from a Half Degree

Many people wonder why a half degree of global warming is such a big deal, especially because Earth has already warmed an entire degree since the 1800s. It is because the rise of another half degree could gravely impact environments and animals. For example, a polar ice melt would lead to a habitat loss for polar bears,

The effects of climate change negatively impact the world's coral reefs and marine life, such as turtles and fish, that live in their protective stretches.

whales, and seals. It would also mean that 23 percent more of the world's population would suffer from extreme heat, and roughly sixty million more people would suffer from drought and water scarcity. With just an extra half degree of warming, coral reefs would cease to exist, sea levels would rise, flooding would worsen, and crop yields would drop. The effects of a half degree of warming could also lead to political unrest as populations would not be affected uniformly. For example, areas such as the Arctic, Mediterranean, and Middle East would be more critically affected, heating up two to three times faster than other locations. Whole communities would be forced to migrate from these countries, putting a strain on resources and infrastructures in their new locations. Such stress could lead to feelings of frustration and anger, and could result in bickering and fighting among nationals and immigrants.

act immediately to cut emissions deeply. In fact, every tenth of a degree matters."

As if the IPCC's climate report wasn't concerning enough, the US Global Change Research Program (USGCRP), under an order from Congress, produced the Fourth National Climate Assessment on November 23, 2018. The USGCRP is a federal program mandated by Congress to coordinate federal research and funding concerning the human and natural forces that shape the environment and impact society. The USGCRP's report, which was the fourth in a series of reports produced for the government, summarized the effects climate change is already having on communities, the economy, ecosystems, water, health, species, agriculture, and infrastructure in the United States. It also made it clear that these impacts were interconnected. According to National Climate Assessment's "Volume II: Impacts, Risks, and Adaptation in the United States: Summary Findings," climate change influences the natural, social, and built systems we rely on. These systems are interconnected and become more vulnerable and unpredictable. The conclusion of the IPCC and USGCRP reports were undeniable: human activity is taking a drastic toll on the health of the planet, and it is imperative that the world's nations take immediate action or 2030 will be too late.

Ecoanxiety Escalating

The reports from the IPCC and the USGCRP elicited a wide variety of reactions from the world's population. Some people were resolved to do more

A Line in the Sand

Many IPCC scientists have spoken about the urgency of the climate change situation. Debra Roberts, part of the IPCC group that contributed to the 2018 report, stated that "[the IPCC report is] a line in the sand and what it says to our species is that this is the moment and we must act now. This is the largest clarion bell from the science community and I hope it mobilizes people and dents the mood of complacency." According to Jonathan Watts's article on TheGuardian.com, Jim Skea, another IPCC scientist, said, "We have presented governments with pretty hard choices. We have pointed out the enormous benefits of keeping to 1.5C, and also the unprecedented shift in energy systems and transport that would be needed to achieve that." Skea added that while the science is there to work on climate change, it would take both the urging of constituents to make important changes and the will of governments to enact impactful policies.

to combat global warming, to take part in climate action groups, and to press their elected officials to pass new policies and legislation. Others read the news with interest but were not inspired to take action. Still, there were those who refused to believe that climate change is a real and proven scientific phenomenon, shrugging off the reports' contents and considering them to be a conspiracy or political ploy. There were even those who responded angrily to the reports. US president Donald Trump didn't believe the findings of the IPCC report. He said, according to BBC.com, "Right now we're at the cleanest we've ever been and that's very important to me." For others, however, the two 2018 reports either created or worsened a psychological reaction to climate change known as ecoanxiety. Worry sets in, fears for the future deepen, and increased symptoms appear. Journalist and meteorologist Eric Holthaus described his experiences with ecoanxiety in a SierraClub.org article. He lost sleep each night, worried about climate change. He couldn't recall how long he had been dealing with the symptoms of ecoanxiety but knew things were getting worse. Holthaus admitted that he needed help and has spent a lot of time "between soul-crushing despair and headstrong hope."

Well before the 2018 reports on climate change, therapists and psychologists were observing the effects of anxiety in their patients, both in those who experienced climate-related catastrophes such as hurricanes, floods, and wildfires, and those who

On April 22, 2012, thousands of Canadians marched through the streets of Vancouver, British Columbia, showing their support during an Earth Day parade.

were overwhelmed by daunting news reports and research on the matter.

The term "ecoanxiety" was first used in 2006, and in March 2017, the American Psychological Association (APA) published a paper titled "Mental Health and Our Changing Climate: Impacts, Implications, and Guidance." It said, in part:

Gradual, long-term changes in climate can also surface a number of different emotions, including fear, anger, feelings of powerlessness, or exhaustion ... Changes in climate affect agriculture, infrastructure and livability, which in turn affect occupations and quality of life and can force people to migrate. These effects may lead to loss of personal and professional identity, loss of social support structures, loss of a sense of control and autonomy and other mental health impacts such as feelings of helplessness, fear and fatalism ... Watching the slow and seemingly irrevocable impacts of climate change unfold, and worrying about the future for oneself, children, and later generations, may be an additional source of stress.

The APA report listed specific acute and chronic mental health effects from climate change. It included the following:

- aggression
- anxiety
- compounded stress
- depression
- fatalism

- fear
- feelings of helplessness
- the loss of autonomy and control
- the loss of personal and occupational identity
- the loss of personally important places
- post-traumatic stress disorder (PTSD)
- strains on social relationships
- substance abuse

Ecoanxiety is a recognized mental health disorder. It can cause symptoms such as depression, fear, feelings of helplessness, and thoughts of suicide.

- suicide
- trauma and shock
- violence

A Real Disorder

Ecoanxiety is a verified mental health issue, identified by psychologists and other mental health professionals. As the climate change news has grown more dire, the number of people suffering from at least some degree of stress as a result is growing. Ecoanxiety is a relatively new health issue, and one that has evolved as the awareness of climate change has grown. To study the evolution of ecoanxiety, it is helpful to review the basics of climate change and how it has grown to be one of the world's most pressing issues.

Myths & FACTS

Myth: Climate change is a natural process that has been taking place for millions of years.

Fact: Scientists agree that climate change is man-made and has brought warm temperatures to higher levels than ever before.

Myth: Ecoanxiety is not a real mental health disorder.

Fact: The APA and the *Diagnostic and Statistical Manual of Mental Disorders (DSM-5)* both state that ecoanxiety is a real mental health issue that may require a professional diagnosis and treatment.

Myth: Everything and everyone will naturally adapt to climate change.

Fact: While some plant and animal species have begun to adapt to climate change, many cannot adapt quickly enough to the changed conditions. Humans may not be able to adapt to changing habitats and locations.

CHAPTER TWO

A Climate Change Review

Ecoanxiety is a fairly "young" mental health condition when compared to other mental health conditions, such as clinical depression, bipolar disorder, and attention deficit hyperactivity disorder (ADHD). It refers to the awareness of climate change as a very real threat to the health of the planet. To understand and learn how to cope with ecoanxiety, one must learn more about the evolution of climate change and its effects. While many people dispute the existence of climate change, the growing number of ecoanxiety cases are linked to the mounting evidence that climate change is a reality.

A Historical Look

Earth has experienced fluctuations in temperatures throughout history, ranging from

Climate change is causing rising temperatures in cold regions. As a result, glaciers in places like Antarctica are melting at an accelerated rate and will eventually lead to rising sea levels.

ice ages to warming periods. In the last 650,000 years, there have been seven cycles. In each instance, a cooling cycle created an ice age. Glaciers began to cover much of the planet but retreated when temperatures warmed. These fluctuations in global temperatures were caused by very small changes in the amount of solar energy received by the planet, which in turn was the result of very small changes in Earth's orbit around the sun. The last ice age ended approximately 7,000 years ago and began what climate scientists call the modern age. It was at this time that human civilization became possible. It is tempting to link today's climate change to just another natural cycle of the planet and the sun, but scientists now know that as much as 95 percent of the warming trend is caused by human activity. Specifically, it can be linked to the level of human activity that has taken place since the nineteenth century. This was a time period known as the Industrial Age, when fossil fuels were used to power machinery and create energy. This practice sent increasing amounts of carbon dioxide into Earth's atmosphere. Carbon dioxide is known as a greenhouse gas because it traps heat in the atmosphere and causes the planet's temperatures to rise. While it is not the only greenhouse gas, carbon dioxide is created by humans and is the most highly produced greenhouse gas. The rate of global warming is at a level that has never before been seen. Since the nineteenth century, the temperature of the planet has risen 1.62°F (0.9°C). Most of this warming has occurred over the last four decades. The warmest year was 2016, with eleven of its twelve months reaching record highs.

Unmistakable Signs

Scientists use various methods to study changes in Earth's atmosphere and its greenhouse gas levels over long periods of time. One of these methods is to examine ice cores harvested from places such as Greenland, Antarctica, and mountaintop glaciers in tropical regions. Ice cores are drilled from ice sheets. Samples from the planet's ancient atmosphere are preserved in their bubbles. Scientists analyze these samples, comparing them to the modern-day rate of warming. Another method used to study changes in the planet's atmosphere is to study tree growth rings, layers of sedimentary rocks, and coral reefs. These, too, offer tangible samples that can be calculated and compared to show the reality of climate change.

Scientists pull Arctic ice core samples in order to research the effects of climate change and ozone depletion in cold regions.

25

The Basics of Greenhouse Gases

While carbon dioxide makes up about 64 percent of the gases created by human activity, there are other greenhouse gases that contribute to climate change. Methane makes up 17 percent of all greenhouse gases and is created from the decay of animal manure, the breakdown of garbage in landfills, the production and transportation of natural gas, and the act of coal mining. Methane remains in the atmosphere for roughly twelve years and traps 20 percent more heat than the same amount of carbon dioxide.

Chlorofluorocarbons (CFCs) make up 12 percent of all greenhouse gases. CFCs stay in the atmosphere for a long time and damage the thin part of Earth's atmosphere known as the ozone layer. The ozone layer absorbs most of the sun's harmful ultraviolet light. Thanks to a global initiative to stop the use of CFCs, the amounts of these greenhouse gases are steadily declining.

Nitrous oxide, another greenhouse gas, contributes about 6 percent to the greenhouse gas total. It is created by some manufacturing processes, the use of fossil fuels, and the use of fertilizer in farming. Nitrous oxide remains in the atmosphere for about 114 years and traps 298 times more heat than the same amount of carbon dioxide.

Fluorinated gases make up .8 percent of greenhouse gases. They are used for cooling and some manufacturing. Fluorinated gases trap up to twenty-three thousand times more heat than carbon dioxide.

While methane, CFCs, nitrous oxide, and fluorinated gases make up a small percentage of the greenhouse gas total, they are also increasing at faster rates than any other gases. As human activity continues in the form of transportation, electricity production, industry, agriculture, and commercial and residential activities, these gases become trapped in Earth's atmosphere. They mix with other atmospheric gases and spread uniformly around the globe, affecting large industrial countries and those that produce fewer greenhouse gases.

Greenhouse Gases Lead to the Greenhouse Effect

Greenhouse gases produce what is known as the greenhouse effect. Normally, Earth absorbs energy from the sun during the day, which heats its surface. As temperatures cool at night, Earth returns this heat into the atmosphere. However, the greenhouse effect occurs when greenhouse gases in the atmosphere absorb this released heat before it can return to outer space, making Earth's

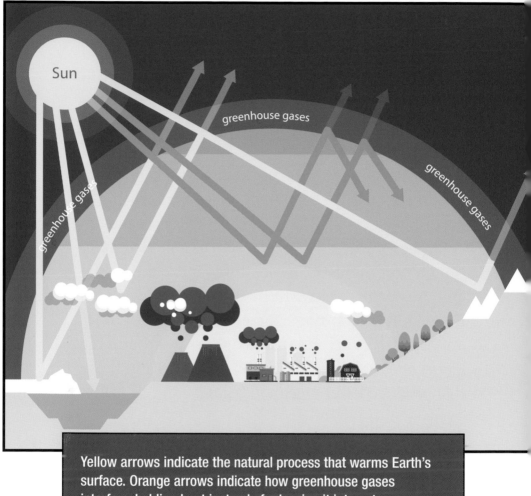

Yellow arrows indicate the natural process that warms Earth's surface. Orange arrows indicate how greenhouse gases interfere, holding heat instead of releasing it into outer space.

atmosphere, and its surface, warmer than usual. The added heat then causes water temperatures on the planet's surface to rise, resulting in water vapor that travels into the atmosphere. Water vapor is also considered to be a greenhouse gas

Carbon by Country

According to the Environmental Protection Agency (EPA)—an independent agency of the US government—the biggest producers of carbon emissions in 2014 were China, the United States, the European Union, India, the Russian Federation, and Japan. Most of their emissions come from fossil fuel burning, natural gas production, and cement manufacturing. Also included in the top twenty list for carbon production were Germany, South Korea, Iran, Canada, Saudi Arabia, Brazil, Mexico, Indonesia, South Africa, the United Kingdom, Australia, Italy, Turkey, France, and Poland. While the production of carbon and greenhouse gases varies greatly from country to country, one cannot escape the greenhouse effect by moving to an undeveloped country. Greenhouse gases mix and disperse equally around Earth's atmosphere, regardless of the level of human activity taking place in a particular area. To make long-lasting strides in climate change, all countries must work together to reduce greenhouse gases and minimize the greenhouse effect.

because it traps heat, which leads to more extreme weather conditions.

Greenhouse gases and a warming atmosphere have a demonstrated negative impact on Earth. A warmer climate leads to warming ocean temperatures, which make storms more powerful and destructive. Shrinking Arctic ice sheets increase sea levels around the world, increasing the likelihood of damaging floods and uninhabitable coastal areas. The loss of snow cover and glaciers affect water supplies and worsen droughts. Higher temperatures also create intense rainfall and catastrophic storms. Carbon dioxide increases the level of acidity in our planet's oceans, which leads to a shortened life span for much of Earth's coral reefs and its marine life.

Living in Denial

Despite the increasing warmth of the planet and growing evidence of the negative impact of climate change, there are still many people who believe that climate change is a hoax and that it doesn't threaten the survival of the planet and its inhabitants. One reason for climate change denial can be traced to the efforts of politicians and lobbyists who have ties to the oil, natural gas, and coal mining industries. These individuals have a deep economic interest in the continued

Politicians and lobbyists with ties to the coal mining industries are among those who do not want industry regulations and deny the existence of climate change.

use of fossil fuels and discourage lawmakers from regulating fossil fuel industries, which would decrease profitability. According to Nicole Mortillaro's article on CBC.ca, Professor Emeritus Paul Thagard from the University of Waterloo in Canada believes:

If you're a conservative politician, you just don't want to believe [in climate change], because if there really is climate change caused by human activity, then there has to be government actions to stop the disastrous results that are probably going to come down the line in 20 or 30 years. There are other fears: people whose livelihood is dependent on, say, the oil industry, might fear acknowledging climate change will threaten their jobs. Others might resent government taking money out of their pockets in the form of public spending on carbon mitigation efforts.

Another reason for climate change denial is that taking aggressive steps to turn things around would require drastic and consistent changes in the high-consumption and material prosperity lifestyles of those living in highly industrialized nations. The level of changes needed per person are almost too much to comprehend and could not be resolved in just a few days, weeks, or months. Even the increasingly frequent occurrence of natural disasters—such as Hurricane Sandy or the wildfires in California—aren't enough to persuade populations to acknowledge what's happening. Denial of climate change, like most forms of denial, is a form of defense by refusing to accept facts in order to protect ourselves from uncomfortable truths. Sara Gorman and Jack M. Gorman noted the following in their PsychologyToday.com article:

> We resist when that calamity is real, will be spread out over decades, and is of catastrophic proportions that can only be averted if we change almost everything about the way we live. Stop driving your car, eating meat, and flying in planes, we are told. Shut down ExxonMobil, Shell, and British Petroleum. Move quickly to build solar fields and energy-producing windmills. Simply writing that list makes us totally exhausted. What we are being asked to do will take gargantuan efforts and face vicious opposition.

Still, many prominent media personalities continue to insist that climate change is a hoax or a myth. Conservative talk show host Rush Limbaugh even accused the US government of exaggerating hurricane forecasts in order to "prove" climate change for political and economic reasons. According to Paul Krugman's article on NYTimes.com, Limbaugh claimed weather scientists manufactured Hurricane Irma's threat to promote the "climate change agenda." He claimed that hurricanes are easy ways to do this, declaring that "fear and panic" cause people to spend

Conservative talk show host Rush Limbaugh has accused the US government of exaggerating severe weather threats in order to prove climate change for political and economic reasons.

lots of money on supplies, such as bottled water, batteries, and advertising.

Working Together

Addressing the changes needed to combat climate change requires a united, global response. Such a response is much more difficult when individuals, companies, and governments refuse to accept that climate change is real. The Paris Agreement, the Kyoto Protocol, and the United Nations 2030 Sustainable Development Goals concerning climate change are all examples of global agreements to cope with climate change. They have also been politically charged and divisive, with some countries refusing to participate. Climate change denial, such as that conveyed by President Trump and other political leaders, reduces the ability of nations to work together and mitigate some of the causes and effects of climate change. For those affected by ecoanxiety, this refusal to believe and act can lead to additional frustrations, stress, and despair.

CHAPTER THREE

The Consequences of a Warmer World

Every news story about a natural disaster, announcement about a newly extinct species, or post about the accelerated loss of ice sheets feeds the fear of those who suffer from ecoanxiety. They have trouble escaping the continuous news feeds of the day, pointing to the ever-present consequences of a world that is warming rapidly.

Weather and Warming

Even for people who do not yet live in a place where droughts or extreme temperatures are already taking place, the signs of a warmer world are occurring more frequently than they once were. Sabrina Stierwalt wrote the following in her ScientificAmerican.com article:

India has suffered from heat waves and extreme droughts, leaving 330 million citizens without enough water to care for their daily needs.

If it feels like we are hearing about extreme weather events more and more frequently now, it's because we are. Large fires are now five times more common and fire season lasts three months longer than 40 years ago. The most intense rainstorms have increased by as much as 70% in the last 50 years and the

37

city of Houston, Texas, has seen three five-hundred-year floods—that is, floods so intense they are only expected to happen once every 500 years—in the last 3 years.

According to the Union of Concerned Scientists, storms that produce the most precipitation—snow or rain—are now producing 20 percent more precipitation that they once were. This is almost three times the rate of increase in total precipitation between 1958 and 2007. Heavy storms are getting even heavier, resulting in record amounts of rain and snow. Just in the northeastern United States, storms are now producing as much as 74 percent more precipitation. This results in flash flooding or debilitating snowfalls, which threaten structures, roads, and bridges, and impact the ability of people to stay warm, stay fed, and be able to work and go to school.

Precipitation amounts aren't the only indicators of a change in weather due to warming. The United States Global Change Research program has noted key points about the changing climate in the nation via its report, *Climate Change Impacts in the United States.* These points include:

- There have been changes in some types of extreme weather events over the last several decades. Heat waves have become more frequent and intense, especially in the West. Cold waves have become less frequent and intense across the nation.

- The intensity, frequency, and duration of North Atlantic hurricanes, as well as the frequency of the strongest (Category 4 and 5) hurricanes, have all increased since the early 1980s.
- Winter storms have increased in frequency and intensity since the 1950s, and their tracks have shifted northward over the United States. Other trends in severe storms, including the intensity and frequency of tornadoes, hail, and damaging thunderstorm winds, are uncertain and are being studied intensively.

Climate change is adding to the severity of weather events that happen naturally. In 2018 alone, there were several major weather events that were exacerbated by climate change: record rainfall amounts and flooding in Japan; record-setting heat waves in many parts of the world, including above the Arctic Circle; terrible wildfires in California, Greece, and Sweden; flooding in India; a typhoon in the Philippines with winds of 165 mph (265.5 kmh); and two record-setting hurricanes, Florence and Michael, that hit the United States. The African city of Ouargla, Algeria, experienced the hottest temperature ever reliably recorded, reaching 124.3°F (51.3°C).

Southern California's drought conditions have led to uncontrollable wildfires that have killed residents and destroyed millions of dollars of property.

The Whys of Warming and Weather

Just how can climate change be linked to incidents of increasingly extreme weather? One analogy for understanding the link is to think about a pot of water being heated on a stove. The heat from the

The Difference Between Weather and Climate

One might be tempted to think climate change isn't real because the weather is "typical" for the season and geographical location. For example, a snowy winter in Toronto, Ontario, would seem normal and unaffected by global warming. However, science has proven that greenhouse gases affect all of us regardless of season and location. The greenhouse effect and consequences of climate change have been found to shake up weather patterns and climate effects, and it is important to understand both individually to get a clear picture of what's happening to our planet.

Weather is the day-to-day state of the atmosphere and is a combination of temperature, humidity, precipitation, cloudiness, visibility, and wind. Weather is usually considered in the short term, because sunny, windy, or stormy conditions are limited to a few days, weeks, or months. Climate, however, is thought to take place in a certain location over a long period of time. Climate is viewed in terms of years, decades, and centuries, and includes statistical weather information about normal weather patterns and the range of weather extremes specific to that area. Scientists generally look for trends and cycles that might indicate longer term or even permanent changes in a climate.

stove does not just heat the water in the pot. It also heats the air around the pot and creates "weather" in the pot, because the water circulates as the heated water rises to the top and the cooler water sinks. The added heat of climate change does the same thing. As the energy trapped by greenhouse gases heat up the air, it also heats up the oceans, melts more ice, and creates more weather.

The increased heat in the atmosphere creates more evaporation, adding water vapor to the atmosphere and intensifying rainfall or snowfall. More evaporation means that soil is drying out, causing droughts and wildfires. Warmer ocean water expands, melting sea ice and creating rising sea levels that cause greater storm surges and flooding. Scientists are also exploring the relationship between melting Arctic ice and colder winters in the northeastern region of the United States, because melting ice weakens the jet stream, allowing colder polar air to travel further south.

The instability of low-level air, which creates thunderstorms, is increased by the warmer and wetter air of climate change. Thunderstorms are then more likely to be severe and cause tornadoes. In addition, these storms may cause more damage on the ground because the air is more buoyant and likely to spawn tornadoes. Much of the worsening weather's link to climate change is because of the hotter air in Earth's atmosphere. In his ScientificAmerican.com article, David Biello quoted climate scientist Kevin Trenberth of the National Center for Atmospheric Research as saying, "The heat has to go somewhere. We expect more extremes in the water cycle in particular. Stronger droughts, bigger heat waves and much greater wildfire risk, but also stronger storms and heavier rainfalls where the rain is occurring. Managing water will be a major challenge."

Past, Present, and Future

One of the reasons why the changing weather contributes to ecoanxiety is that Earth's population has to deal with past and current weather effects, as well as an uncertain future. Climate change is an area where scientists are only beginning to see links between the causes and effects of warming, and no one is certain just what may be coming.

Since climate change became a serious and increasingly visible issue, most people have experienced the real effects of global warming. Over the last decade, climate growing zones have shifted. Some areas have seen more frost and snowfall, while others have seen longer temperate growing seasons. In some parts of the world, droughts or floods have led to a decrease in agricultural production. While some places have seen higher crop yields from

A shift in growing seasons has forced farmers around the world to rethink their regular lineup of plants. They opt for plants and produce that can withstand extreme weather conditions.

the warmer temperatures and increased carbon dioxide in the atmosphere, soil moisture and water availability have decreased yields in other locations. Some farmers have had to change what they grow, substituting higher temperature crops for those that can't survive in a warmer environment. Livestock can be at risk in hotter temperatures, which decreases the food supply. The fishing industry suffers because changes in water temperature make waters more hospitable to invasive species and thus shift the ranges or life cycle timing of certain fish species. The shifting of the habitat areas of fish and shellfish can also disrupt ocean ecosystems. Ultimately, these changes in agricultural yield are expected to affect the natural food chain, as well as the availability, quality, and amount of food available to people all over the world. Increasing difficulty in transporting food to where it is needed, because of weather events, will likely cause higher prices and make contamination and the spoilage of food more common. Famines are already occurring and could increase as food supplies become less stable.

Changing climate attributes are expected to cause significant shifts in populations. Many people have been forced to leave their homes and find new places to live because of coastal flooding, drought, and changing patterns of weather and crop yields. This movement is

A Different New England?

The New England region of the United States is an example of an area that has already experienced many shifts caused by climate change. These range from a two-week decrease in the number of days with temperatures below 32°F (0°C); an increase in annual precipitation; a decrease in the number of snow-covered days in northern New Hampshire and Vermont; a growing season that is now two to three weeks longer; and ice-out dates occurring seven to ten days earlier than in the past. Some traditional New England crops, such as maple trees that produce maple syrup, are no longer growing well in warmer temperatures. New England states that depend on winter sports, such as skiing, are experiencing a loss in tourist revenue. Even the region's famous fall foliage is dulling in color as tree species die and others struggle.

known as climate migration. In some cases, the people who migrate to new areas are referred to as climate refugees, which is similar to the idea of political refugees who are forced to flee their home countries because of violence, war, and oppressive governments. There are many cases of climate migration taking place around the world. In 2018, the World Bank released a report saying that climate change could drive more than 140 million people to migrate within Sub-Saharan Africa, Latin America, and South Asia by the middle of this century. The United Nations stated that by 2045, a similar number of people will be forced to migrate all over the world because of desertification, where areas that once supported agriculture are transformed into dry deserts.

For the first time, the United States used federal funds to relocate people in 2016. Isle de Jean Charles, in southeastern Louisiana, lost much of its land mass because of storms and rising sea levels. Seawater saturated the soil, which made it impossible to grow crops. The wild animals disappeared, and the island was routinely cut off when high tides flooded the only access road from the mainland. Knowing that the island would eventually be overcome with water, the US government gave the island a $48 million grant to relocate all sixty residents to a new community on the mainland. Scientists are also keeping an eye on other coastal cities that could become

In 2018, heavy monsoons and flooding took its toll on Dhaka, the capital city of Bangladesh, making it nearly impossible for residents to navigate the city's waterlogged streets.

uninhabitable as a result of rising sea levels. These include US cities such as Boston, New York, Atlantic City, Charleston, and Miami.

Climate migration also occurs on a global scale. People in Bangladesh left their flooded coastal towns and moved to the capital city of Dhaka at the rate of four hundred thousand a year. They escaped rising sea levels, increased salt water, destructive floods, and cyclones. Freshwater was no longer available, and women and children were forced to walk for hours every day in search of drinkable water. However, Dhaka itself may be at risk for flooding as sea levels continue to rise, which will lead to further climate migration for city dwellers. Climate migration has also increased in areas where intense heat waves have made it unbearable to work outdoors. China, India, and the Middle

Endangered species, like this rare pink dolphin found in the Amazon River, are under additional threat. A severe drought, brought on by climate change, diminished its food supply of fish.

East have all been affected, and the United States is expected to join the list. David Wallace-Wells noted the following in his NYMag.com article:

> *According to an assessment focused only on effects within the U.S. from the National Oceanic and Atmospheric Administration, summer labor of any kind would become impossible in the lower Mississippi Valley, and everybody in the country east of the Rockies would be under more heat stress than anyone, anywhere, in the world today. As Joseph Romm has put it in his authoritative primer* Climate Change: What Everyone Needs to Know, *heat stress in New York City would exceed that of present-day Bahrain, one of the planet's hottest spots.*

Climate change will also cause the extinction of many species of animals, plants, and insects. More than twenty-five thousand species, almost a third of those known, are in danger of disappearing. According to Elizabeth Kolbert's book, *The Sixth Extinction*, "It is estimated that one-third of corals, freshwater mollusks, sharks, and rays, one-fourth of all mammals, one-fifth of all reptiles, and one-sixth of all birds are heading towards extinction." Snow leopards, African antelope, monk seals, river dolphins, and the North American ash tree are already threatened.

Clearly, the world is at risk from climate change. As the severity of climate change and its effects become more evident, many of the world's population have begun to feel anxious about the future of the planet and mankind itself. In response to the rising levels of anxiety regarding climate change, mental health experts have been forced to formalize and treat ecoanxiety as a real mental health issue.

CHAPTER FOUR

The Effect of Climate Change on Mental Health

Ecoanxiety, like other anxiety disorders, is more than everyday feelings of stress or sadness. The National Institute of Mental Health notes the following on its website:

> *Occasional anxiety is an expected part of life. You might feel anxious when faced with a problem at work, before taking a test, or before making an important decision. But anxiety disorders involve more than temporary worry or fear. For a person with an anxiety disorder, the anxiety does not go away and can get worse over time. The symptoms can interfere with daily*

Volunteering in planet-saving activities is one way to cope with ecoanxiety. It helps people feel good about their contributions and connects them with like-minded community members.

activities such as job performance, school work, and relationships.

Anxiety disorders involve excessive worry on a daily basis and persist for a minimum of six months. If left untreated, anxiety disorders can lead to physical symptoms, such as fatigue, restlessness, muscle tension, and difficulty with focus and concentration.

There are several types of anxiety disorders, such as generalized anxiety disorder (GAD), obsessive-compulsive disorder (OCD), panic disorder, post-traumatic stress disorder (PTSD), and social phobia (also known as social anxiety disorder). GAD is chronic anxiety and exaggerated tension and worry, which is based on little to no provocation. OCD is characterized by the repetition of unwanted thoughts and/or behaviors, such as repeated hand washing or counting the times one turns on or off the lights. Panic disorders are sudden, unexpected, recurring panic attacks. They involve a period of intense fear, which may come out of nowhere or may be triggered by fear of an object or a situation. Symptoms include heart palpitations, a pounding or accelerated heartbeat, sweating, shaking, feeling short of breath or as if one is choking, or a feeling of impending doom or being out of control. People who suffer from panic disorders begin to avoid places or situations that might trigger an attack, which

Anxiety disorders, such as ecoanxiety, are often treated with a technique called talk therapy. Patients are invited to talk about their feelings with a trained psychotherapist.

can interfere with normal life. PTSD often develops after one experiences a traumatic event, sometimes involving threats, natural disasters, accidents, or physical harm. Social phobias are brought on by an excessive self-consciousness in typical social situations, such as public speaking or having a meal in front of others. People with a social phobia make every effort to avoid situations in which their symptoms will flare.

Anxiety disorders are usually treated with therapy, such as psychotherapy or talk therapy. This involves the patient speaking with a therapist about their specific disorder. Cognitive behavioral therapy (CBT) is

Chronic Stress and Cortisol

Scientists have known for a long time that high levels of stress produce a hormone called cortisol. Cortisol, in high levels, interferes with learning and memory. It also lowers the body's immune system and bone density, causes an increased amount of weight gain, elevates the blood pressure and cholesterol, and increases the risk of heart disease. Chronic stress, and the resulting high levels of cortisol, lead to a lower life expectancy, as well as increased risks of depression and mental illness. For people suffering from ecoanxiety, their constant anxiety over climate change and possible catastrophes puts them at risk from higher cortisol levels. This is particularly true for young people, as scientific studies have linked elevated cortisol levels as being more likely in adolescence. Millennials—those who became young adults in the early twenty-first century—are particularly susceptible to suffer from ecoanxiety.

another method, in which the patient works with a therapist to learn new ways of thinking, behaving, and reacting to the objects and situations that trigger their anxieties. Some patients are also given antianxiety medications to help them manage the symptoms of fear and anxiety.

The Daily Fear

An anxiety disorder that is related to the actual and perceived fate of the planet may seem less severe in scope than an anxiety disorder related to a fear of dogs or social situations. For those who experience ecoanxiety, however, it is a very real condition that affects their daily lives. Liz Galst, an editorial consultant who lives in New York City, deals with ecoanxiety and the fear of climate change every day. According to a CBC.ca article:

> "I'm anxious all the time. I don't have a way to stop being anxious. Nobody around seems to be anxious about [climate change]. In fact, nobody around seems to be concerned at all about it." Galst worries in bed late into the night, obsessing about everything. She takes the stairs to save "every last bit of electricity" and hands out cards to idling motorists explaining the benefits of turning their engines off. She even hassles her friends about switching to renewable energy sources. But nothing she does relieves her anxiety. "I

keep telling myself to try and calm down, and at the same time I keep telling myself there must be something more that I can do."

Ecoanxiety is especially common with millennials, as they grew up watching negative media reports on the environment. The Harris Poll, which was featured in an April 2018 PRNewswire .com article, lists the following:

- *92% of Americans are worried about the future of our planet*
- *Nearly three quarters (72%) of millennials 18–34 say that watching, hearing and/or reading negative news stories about the environment sometimes has an impact on their emotional wellbeing (e.g., anxiety, racing thoughts, sleep problems, a feeling of uneasiness)*
- *Among those who say they are worried about the future of our planet, about two-thirds say they take steps to reduce energy use in their home (68%) or take steps to reduce water waste in their home (64%)*
- *Only 13% of American adults invest in environmentally responsible*

companies to address worries about the future of the planet, but millennials are ahead of the curve with 20% investing in companies that prioritize the environment.

Progressive Stages of Ecoanxiety

Ecoanxiety develops in progressive stages. In the first stage, denial, people avoid any acknowledging that a problem exists. Then, as people become more consciously aware of the issue, they move on to Stage 2, semi-consciousness. Stage 3 is described as a moment of realization. Such a moment might occur when reading a compelling article or when personally experiencing the negative impacts of climate change, such as a natural disaster. Once people "wake up" to the threats that Earth is facing and reach a so-called "point of no return," also known as Stage 4, they typically experience feelings of despair, hopelessness, and guilt in Stage 5. This is followed by the final stage of acceptance and action, in which people take steps to help the environment and live a more sustainable lifestyle.

It's during Stage 4 that ecoanxiety can, like other anxiety disorders, manifest itself with both mental and physical symptoms. Most of these symptoms are

Eco Extreme: Ecoterrorism

Climate change has also created a new breed of terrorism, known as ecoterrorism. Ecoterrorist groups, such as Earth First! and Earth Liberation Front (ELF), practice what they call "ecotage," the combined

(continued on next page)

On March 15, 2009, young protesters all over the world skipped school to encourage world leaders to take action against climate change and government inaction.

(continued from the previous page)

wordplay of "eco" and "sabotage." These acts have included burning down multimillion-dollar luxury homes, ski resorts, and other structures that seem to be a threat to the ecosystems they are built on. They also vandalized or burned SUVs, construction equipment, and genetically engineered crops. Ecoterrorists also place spikes on roads, disable vehicles, vandalize homes, and deliver sewage or dead animals to corporate offices. While this kind of terrorism has not yet involved injuring or killing humans, there is the fear that their activities will escalate to that level. People who belong to environmental groups that do not promote ecoterrorism also fear that all environmental groups will get a bad name from these terrorist activities. Since 1976, ecoterrorism groups have committed 1,100 terrorist acts, causing more than $110 million of damage. The FBI now lists ecoterrorists as the number one domestic terror threat in the United States.

similar to general anxiety disorders, including panic attacks, insomnia, nightmares, grief, helplessness, depression, and irritability. Those with ecoanxiety may burst into tears when they see news items about extinct animals or melting ice sheets. Physical symptoms may include physical pain, unexplained weakness, and loss of appetite. In extreme cases, ecoanxiety sufferers may even feel rage.

For people who survive natural disasters brought on by a changing climate, the initial terror, anger, shock, fear, and grief over lost loved ones can become PTSD, as well as anxiety and mood disorders. After Hurricane Katrina struck New Orleans, Louisiana, in 2005 and Hurricane Sandy struck the East Coast in 2012, many residents of those areas had symptoms of PTSD. The rates of suicide rose as well.

Media Makes It Worse

Psychologists believe that one of the reasons why ecoanxiety is growing is due to the vast amount of information about climate change and impending catastrophes in the media. Stories are printed in newspapers, written about in government climate reports, and featured on social media with increasing frequency. Rebecca Fearn's article on Bustle.com quoted psychologist Honey Langcaster-James as saying, "The [mainstream] media, and the sharing of distressing and concerning material by friends on social media, can heighten the anxiety some people feel and this can lead to an overwhelming fear that may well be disproportionate." In addition to media

Although it's impossible to fully escape negative news about the environment, there is a wealth of online resources designed to help you maintain a positive outlook on life.

publications, climate change is also dominant in academic curricula, political debates, and election platforms—all of which make it a difficult topic to avoid. Langcaster-James pointed out that millennials are especially affected by the focus on environmental issues: "Negative news affects millennials more than other generations because they're so interconnected. They've grown up with the latest news and social media updates available in the palm of their hand all the time. That means it's impossible to escape, and they can also feel connected to the struggles of those thousands of miles away."

Ecoanxiety is now a recognized anxiety disorder, according to the APA, and its occurrence is expected to increase as climate change becomes more dire and more prominent in communications. With more and more people likely to suffer from ecoanxiety, it is important to know how to recognize the triggers in order to cope with the symptoms.

CHAPTER FIVE

What to Do About Ecoanxiety

The first step in coping with ecoanxiety is to acknowledge that it exists and to take it seriously. Avoid the temptation to suppress or minimize the fears you or someone you care about might be experiencing. This is especially important for those who have already experienced a hurricane, a drought, or extreme higher temperatures. It is also important for those who already suffer from another type of anxiety disorder, which can intensify if coupled with ecoanxiety.

Are You at Risk?

It is normal to wonder if you are at risk for, or already suffer from, ecoanxiety. Young people, in particular, endure a higher incidence of ecoanxiety as they are considered to be the first generation

One way to effectively deal with ecoanxiety is to acknowledge that it exists. Many students find it helpful to talk with others who are experiencing the same emotions.

to have grown up with and experienced the real signs of an impending climate crisis. Many are even questioning whether or not to have children in this new climate reality. It is not difficult to see why they ponder the state of their mental health and make decisions that shape their futures, as they have experienced the greatest amount of news and information—both real and embellished—than any other generation. Tina Yeonju Oh, a graduate student in environmental studies, recalled the night of President Trump's election on November 8, 2016. Her reaction is explained in Steph Wechsler's article on NationalObserver.com:

> *Oh was in Marrakesh, Morocco, for the United Nations climate conference following the Paris Agreement. She and some others at the conference had not expected Trump's win. "I have never felt grief like that before." She recalls being unable to eat or sleep. "I think it was compounded by the fact that I was in a space where we were talking about the urgency of climate change and how immediately and how big the effects would*

To deal with the stress of ecoanxiety, consider participating in outdoor activities that have a positive effect on the environment.

be for marginalized communities all over the world. And just feeling the weight of the most powerful politician in the world be a climate denier."

Oh and others of the millennial generation are not alone in their concerns. Other generations experience ecoanxiety, affecting their thoughts for now and the future. According to Steph Wechsler, Dr. Courtney Howard explained, "Climate-related events have started to shift people's thoughts away from thinking of climate change as something that has to do with carbon dioxide on a graph and something that has to do with them and their children and their health and their future."

First Steps

One very basic way to cope with ecoanxiety is to talk with others about the symptoms. Options can include a parent or guardian, teacher, counselor, spiritual leader, mentor, or friend. People who suffer from ecoanxiety, but isolate themselves and keep their fears private, tend to suffer more severe symptoms. Steph Wechsler quoted Dr. Howard as stating: "[Climate anxiety] can be alienating. You can think to yourself, 'well, what's wrong with me? Maybe I shouldn't worry about it so much.'

If we talk about it, we may still feel sad, but we don't have to feel lonely and we don't have to feel like those feelings make us odd. In fact, it's very normal to be anxious and scared if there's a threat."

Other steps to cope with ecoanxiety is for sufferers to practice "self-care." This technique includes self-observance and tending to one's needs with intentional care, such as going to bed early and getting enough rest, eating a healthy diet, and exercising on a regular basis. It can also include taking part in more outdoor activities, such as gardening, walking, or hiking. Self-care practices can be quick and easy, such as taking a break from technology, television, and social media, or participating in meaningful meditation or yoga.

Getting More Help

For some people suffering from ecoanxiety, the help of a professional therapist is needed to cope with serious symptoms. These specialists employ a process called ecotherapy, which is a treatment program that connects humans with nature to improve mental and physical well-being. In the early 1990s, a historian and sociologist named Theodor Roszak popularized the term "ecopsychology" to discuss the conflict and mental health issues

Many people feel separated from nature. To promote connection, some ecoanxiety therapies require patients to spend quality time in natural settings.

that were developing around the environment. Ecopsychology is based on the idea that the physical and emotional health and well-being of a patient is based on the relationship of people to the planet. If this relationship is disrupted in any way, it can lead to stress and anxiety for the patient. Ecopsychology explores people's upbringing, which can affect their

People and Their Environment

GoodTherapy.org described the effect of the environment on people via a study conducted by psychologist Terry Hartig:

> Participants were asked to complete a 40-minute cognitive task designed to induce mental fatigue. Following the task, participants were randomly assigned 40 minutes of time to be spent in one of three conditions: walking in a nature preserve, walking in an urban area, or sitting quietly while reading magazines and listening to music. Participants who had walked in the nature preserve reported less anger and more positive emotions than those who engaged in the other activities. In a similar study conducted by Mind, a mental health charity organization, a nature walk reduced symptoms of depression in 71% of participants, compared to only 45% of those who took a walk through a shopping center.

relationship to the environment. It also takes a look at their carbon footprint and what they might be able to do to help the environment come back from a threatened future.

Another ecopsychologist, Michael J. Cohen, developed an approach called natural thinking systems process (NTSP). This system is based on the idea that anxiety is rooted in a deep disconnect between human health and the health of the planet. According to Michael J. Cohen's article in Edpsych .com, "Biologically and psychologically we are part of nature and nature is part of us. Survival demands that we and Mother Nature mutually fulfill each other's needs. However, we live in extreme separation from nature and its balanced ways." It is only by reconnecting with nature that people can heal their anxiety. Cohen's NTSP therapies include outdoor activities where patients experience nature and then consider the connections that people and nature need for healthy outcomes.

The Nature-Based Therapy of Ecotherapy

Ecotherapy is a blanket term for a wide variety of nature-based healing approaches. Some therapies take place between the therapist and patient, while others take place in a group setting. Most often, ecotherapy sessions are held outdoors. Patients are encouraged to consider their emotional responses to the natural world and explore the way they felt about nature as children. They recall outdoor memories in the hopes of renewing their connection to nature. This helps patients feel as if they're in control of making positive changes for the environment.

Ecotherapists also urge patients to garden or visit a park on a regular basis. They also suggest "forest bathing," which is the act of simply being in nature. This could involve mindful meditation or being thoughtfully aware of one's surroundings, but physical activities can be saved for another time. These activities would include hiking, bicycling, or another activity to focus on fitness. Ecotherapists may even urge patients to carry a small token symbolizing nature. A rock, shell, or feather—carrying these on a regular basis reinforces a connection to nature, regardless of the environment patients find themselves in.

Ecotherapists also explore the environmental stewardship habits that patients might have practiced during childhood. Perhaps their families recycled and practiced energy reduction methods, such as turning off lights or upgrading appliances to energy-saving models. If so, these lasting patterns can be highlighted to help patients see that they have contributed to the health of the planet. Patients may see how these acts developed into habits they still maintain and realize how their example of healthy stewardship inspired the values, attitudes, and behaviors of others in a similar way. This technique gives patients feelings of control over their situation, helping them to see that both individuals and the environment are capable of resilience. Patients feel that their efforts to help the planet do matter, are meaningful, and have wide-reaching impact.

Beyond Therapy

People who suffer from ecoanxiety find comfort in ecofriendly habits. These habits can include small steps, such as recycling, reducing waste, composting, using reusable shopping bags, and buying ecofriendly products such as LED light bulbs and products made with minimal plastic packaging. Consumers can choose to buy goods and services from companies with a commitment to green practices and products. (Investing in such companies is a great way to support the cause.) Emergency plans might provide peace of mind, helping those with ecoanxiety to feel as if they are prepared to handle natural disasters that might arise because of the changing climate and

Another way to cope with ecoanxiety is to be prepared for all sorts of weather situations. Consider putting together an emergency kit or picking one up from a local organization.

weather patterns. Training is available for those who want to learn how to act in the event of a disaster or life-changing catastrophe. Ecofriendly habits can be applied to even more significant commitments, such as adopting a vegetarian diet, using public transportation, and limiting car and airline travel. Families may even decide to have fewer children to reduce their carbon footprint.

Group participation on a non-therapy basis is also helpful when coping with ecoanxiety. Conservation activities that welcome volunteers to plant trees or restore habitats are a great way to help the environment and reestablish a connection to the earth. Neighborhood groups dedicated to maintaining community green spaces or gardens, or establishing better recycling programs are also beneficial, with the added advantage of reducing the sense of isolation that ecoanxiety can create. It can also be helpful to contribute money to organizations that exist to benefit the planet, as well as urging politicians to enact environmentally friendly laws or enact environmental protection legislation.

Above all, it is important to understand that any change or effort made for the betterment of the environment is valuable. Below are some points to keep in mind:

- We can only change what's within our capability, such as money, location, job, and family demands.
- Because it's not easy to change habits and routines, we should not beat ourselves up or feel guilty about the things we cannot do.

The fact that we want to make a change is worth celebrating.
- Small changes are just as important as grand statements.

The strongest ways to cope with a changing planet is to build strong social networks of family, friends, and community, and to cultivate a sense of optimism. It may not feel as if one person alone can make a difference, but the power of millions of people, each making small changes, can be enormous.

10 Great Questions to Ask an Ecotherapist

1. Is ecoanxiety a real mental health disorder?

2. What is the most important thing I can do if I think I have ecoanxiety?

3. What are the main symptoms of ecoanxiety?

4. At what point do I need to get help from an ecotherapist?

5. What are the main treatments for ecoanxiety?

6. Why does reconnecting with nature help ecoanxiety?

7. What can one person do to make a difference regarding climate change?

8. What can I do to help a friend or family member who is suffering from ecoanxiety?

9. Can kids get ecoanxiety? Are there special treatments just for them?

10. What can I do to help myself from becoming ecoanxious?

CHAPTER SIX

The Next Steps

Ecoanxiety can be a very individual condition, but there are things that can be done to reach out and involve a broader community for help and healing.

Power in Numbers

Just as millions of people make small lifestyle decisions every day, large organizations have the power to create change in a big way when they team up with helping hands. This is called a collection action, and it can go a long way in helping the planet and easing the mind of those with ecoanxiety. One such collection action is the REACH-NOLA, which stands for the Rapid Evaluation and Action for Community Health in New Orleans, Louisiana. REACH-NOLA was founded in 2006 as a response to the aftermath of Hurricane Katrina in 2005.

After Hurricane Katrina, only a limited number of mental health professionals remained in the area. This made it especially difficult for survivors to receive help for their ecoanxiety.

This devastating storm left many people in New Orleans, Louisiana, with mental health issues and only a few of the city's doctors and mental health professionals to turn to. Most had already left the area due to the hurricane's damage. The lack of resources was especially harmful to those who lived in low-income areas. REACH-NOLA stepped up to help. They reached out to the remaining populations to help them cope with the trauma, PTSD, and ecoanxiety. They also established a partnership between community-based programs and academic institutions, and developed a network of quality health care programs with partners, services, and research. Community health clinics and hospitals united forces with university research centers to create mental health services that were accessible to everyone. These steps went a long way in helping hurricane survivors.

The Transition Towns Movement is a community-based program that helps people deal with the impacts of climate change. It encourages participants to work together to build resilience.

The Transition Towns Movement is another community-based initiative that helps people deal with the impacts of climate change. It is a grassroots program, in which members of a specific area work together to build their community's resilience to the effects of climate change, fossil fuels, and economic issues. Transition Towns are located around the world, including the United States, Canada, the United Kingdom, Italy, and Chile. Transition Town organizations are different from other groups that focus on sustainability and the environment because they also concentrate on personal commitment, coping, and citizen-led education and action. An article on TransitionUS.org notes the following:

> *It all starts off when a small collection of motivated individuals within a community come together with a shared concern: How can our community respond to the challenges and opportunities of peak oil, climate change and the economic crisis? This small team of people begin by forming an initiating group and then adopt the Transition Model with the intention of engaging a significant proportion of the people in their community to kick off a Transition Initiative.*

Working together, and using the organizational and training materials provided by the Transition United States organization (or other groups around the world) in their Transition Handbook and framework, the community begins to address questions like how to create resilience within all the systems that a community needs to survive and

Indigenous Communities

Indigenous people around the world are often among those who are most impacted by the effects of climate change. Desert communities suffer from droughts and a lack of drinking water. Communities in the Himalayas cope with more-than-usual snow melt and fluctuating water supplies. People who live in the Arctic region experience a loss of traditional food sources, and poor ice and weather conditions make it unsafe to travel and difficult to hunt. Conversely, many indigenous communities have come up with creative ways to cope with their changing situations. In Bangladesh, communities created floating gardens to prevent their crops from destructive floods. People in Vietnam planted mangroves along the coast to reduce the effects of tropical storm waves. Indigenous farmers around the world swapped out their crops in favor of more climate-friendly produce. Indigenous communities may be affected much more than other communities, but they also demonstrate great resilience in adversity.

thrive, how to reduce carbon emissions, and how to create a good local economy to better handle larger national and global economic challenges. Although the term "transition towns" is commonly used, this process works for "Transition Cities, Transition Islands, Transition Hamlets, Transition Valleys, Transition Anywhere-You-Find-People." Transition United States also has a Youth Mentors program, in which teens can become involved

Indigenous agricultural communities are greatly affected by climate change. They demonstrate resilience by finding new ways to grow and harvest valuable food resources.

with their community's transition plan, support older community members, and mentor their peers. Sam Rossiter wrote the following in his TransitionNetwork.org article:

> *The challenges our societies and their young people face are numerous and varied; from rising seas and food prices, to precarious work and loss of traditional cultures. So, although it is in human nature to think that now is the critical moment, with climate breakdown happening around us I believe my generation has really inherited a unique challenge. We don't have the luxury of waiting until we're older and more experienced to make change happen, which makes the support of peers and elders all the more vital.*

The Next Level

Beyond the community level, individuals concerned with climate change and solutions to ecoanxiety can find relief by participating in organizations and actions on the state and national levels. Governments on both levels are responsible for many of the widespread policies and laws that concern climate change, the environment, and emissions. Both individuals and representatives of large corporations and organizations lobby the government on a continual basis, trying to persuade lawmakers to enact legislation in favor of the planet. Unfortunately, the groups of lobbyists with the most money to spend on persuading lawmakers are the representatives of big businesses, such as those in the electrical utilities sector, fossil fuel companies, and transportation corporations. These companies often oppose legislation that would benefit the environment or slow climate change in some way, simply because those measures cost them money. It is imperative that regular citizens spend time reaching out to their representatives at both the state and national level, to lend their voice to pro-environmental initiatives and their vote to those who represent such movements. This kind of activism not only helps to sway policy decisions, but it helps those who suffer from ecoanxiety feel more powerful in taking a stand against negative government action against the environment. As with any form of action, there is power in the collective voice of people of those who stand together in solidarity, make their wishes known to elected politicians, and use their voting power to put representatives in place with an agenda that addresses climate change.

States That Are Leading the Way

In July 2017, then-governor Edmund G. Brown Jr. of California signed air quality and climate legislation to extend and improve his state's market-based cap-and-trade program to 2030. Cap-and-trade is a system for reducing air pollution. It sets limits on the amount of greenhouse gas emissions (the cap) and lets companies that don't use up all their emission allowance to sell their extra allowance to other companies (the trade). California has one of the most aggressive plans for reducing carbon emissions: a 40 percent reduction in carbon below the levels in place in 1990. The legislation also authorizes the state to use money from the cap-and-trade program to fund clean energy development, particularly in disadvantaged communities. According to a CA.gov article, California's senate president pro tempore Kevin de León stated that "the world is looking to California. We are proving that growing an economy and protecting the environment is not an either-or proposition; we can and will continue to do both. Today's extension of our landmark cap-and-trade program, coupled with our effective clean energy policies, will move us forward into the future and we plan to take the rest of the world with us."

California's success story shows that state government can make a huge difference in climate issues and that there is power in people who elect

Government initiatives, such as reducing food waste and using compost as an energy source, can make a significant difference when dealing with climate issues.

officials with ecofriendly agendas. Other states are taking similar steps. In 2018, the people of Nevada voted to increase the renewable energy portfolio standard for state utilities from 15 percent in 2025 to 50 percent by 2030. Their goal was to produce more power from renewable sources and less from fossil fuels. In 2017, New Jersey enacted legislation aimed at reducing food waste by 50 percent by the 2030. This effort keeps food waste out of landfills and garbage dumps, which reduces the amount of methane that is produced as the food rots. Plus, the food waste can be converted into energy to power homes across the state.

A Look Toward the Federal Government

Citizens can also let their representatives in the national government know that they support global climate change initiatives, such as the Paris Agreement. The agreement is a pledge by certain countries to keep climate warming levels at just 3.6°F (2°C) and to increase the abilities of countries to deal with the impacts brought on by climate change. As President Trump has vowed to pull the United States out of this agreement, governments on local and state levels have intensified their efforts to support and enact the clean energy advances needed to meet the goals of the accord and slow dangerous climate change. Again, it is within the power of individuals to let their elected lawmakers know what they think about climate change, and lower level governments can make a difference.

Carbon, Carbon, and More Carbon

States and countries are enacting ideas for taxing and reducing carbon emissions. One such country is Canada. In 2018, it enacted a carbon fee and

Climate and Communities

Climate change affects communities in many ways. These changes include a loss of culture and a loss of employment. According to an article on ClimateChangeConnection.org, "Climate change will have physical, social and cultural impacts on cultural heritage." For example, archaeological evidence, historical buildings, monuments, and other heritage sites will be directly affected by changes in weather patterns and indirectly by society's changing values. Although loss of employment may be considered an economic impact of climate change, unemployment, particularly in resource-based communities such as forestry and fishing, can affect all aspects of community life. On a personal level, unemployment can increase family stress, and on a community level, recreation programs may suffer as families leave the community in search of employment elsewhere.

dividend program, in which companies are charged a tax on carbon, starting at $20 per ton in 2019. Charges are set to rise annually at $10 per ton until

CLIMATE ACTION **NOW**
—
AGISSONS **MAINTENANT**
POUR LE CLIMAT

Under Prime Minister Justin Trudeau, Canada has enacted a carbon fee and dividend program that taxes carbon. The goal is to reduce the nation's carbon emissions.

the rate reaches $50 per ton in 2022. The money raised by this tax will be returned to Canadian taxpayers in provinces that don't already have carbon pricing systems in their provincial level. According to a CitizensClimateLobby.org article, Canadian prime minister Justin Trudeau said, "It is free to pollute, so we have too much pollution. Starting next year, it will no longer be free to pollute anywhere in Canada. We are going to place a price on the pollution that causes climate change from coast to coast to coast."

Carbon pricing, which is the term used for policies such as carbon taxing and cap-and-trade programs, is generally seen as the best way for the world to control carbon emissions. They also include other complementary policies, many of which consumers just like you can participate in. Examples of policies can vary, such as setting fuel efficiency standards for buildings and vehicles, offering tax exemptions for appliances and energy efficiency improvements, requiring energy utilities to use a certain amount of renewable energy in their power generation, and enforcing existing laws on energy and environmental protection. Government policies can even include reducing tariffs on green goods, such as solar panels, wind turbines, and energy-efficient light bulbs, so that these things are less expensive for consumers.

As today's world gets warmer and more volatile, it is easy for everyone to feel different degrees of ecoanxiety about our future and the future of our shared plant. While ecoanxiety may feel personal and make people feel helpless, there are places to go for personal help in coping with those feelings. It is also important to remember that as a group of consumers, media, lawyers, and politicians working together, changes can be made to help us participate in building a better future. None of us are powerless.

acute Taking place at a severe or intense degree.

atmosphere The envelope of gases that surrounds a planet such as Earth.

chronic Reoccurring or lasting a long time.

composting The act of collecting organic matter (e.g., vegetable peels, grass, and leaves) and allowing it to decay in order to fertilize soil.

ecofriendly Not harmful to the environment.

ecopsychology The study of the relationship between human beings and the natural world.

fluctuation An unpredictable rising and falling or change in the level or amount of something.

grassroots Having to do with the ordinary people in an organization or society, rather than the elite or the leadership.

greenhouse gas A gas, such as carbon dioxide, that contributes to the greenhouse effect warming the planet.

habitat The natural environment of a plant, animal, or other organism.

ice-out date The date when a large lake is officially declared free of ice.

impending About to happen.

indigenous Native or original to a region.

infrastructure The physical structures of a place, such as bridges and roads, that are needed for functionality.

lobbyist Someone whose job it is to persuade or influence legislators.

migrate To move from one location to another.

palpitation A very strong, rapid, or irregular heartbeat due to stress or exertion.

phobia An extreme or irrational fear of something.

ratified Formally sanctioned or approved, such as a contract or treaty.

resilience The ability of someone or something to recover quickly from difficulties.

stewardship The role or ability to take care of something, such as the environment.

storm surge An abnormal rise in the level of the ocean tide due to a storm.

sustainable Able to continue for a long time and cause little or no damage to the environment.

For More Information

American Psychological Association (APA)

750 First Street NE

Washington, DC 20002-4242

(800) 374-2721

Website: www.apa.org

Facebook: @AmericanPsychologicalAssociation

Twitter: @APA

YouTube: American Psychological Association

The APA is the leading scientific and professional organization representing psychology in the United States. It establishes standards and promotes psychology and psychological knowledge.

Canadian Psychological Association (CPA)

141 Laurier Avenue West, Suite 702

Ottawa, ON K1P 5J3

Canada

(613) 237-2144

Website: https://cpa.ca

Facebook: @CPA.SCP

Twitter: @CPA_SCP

YouTube: CPAVideoChannel

Email: cpa@cpa.ca

CPA's mission is to improve the health and well-being of all Canadians and to promote the advancement, development, dissemination, and application of psychological knowledge. It also provides support for psychology professionals across the country.

Citizens' Climate Lobby

1330 Orange Avenue #309

Coronado, CA 92118

(619) 437-7142

Website: www.citizensclimatelobby.org

Facebook: @CitizensClimateLobby

Instagram and Twitter: @citizensclimate

YouTube: Citizens' Climate Lobby

The Citizens' Climate Lobby is a nonprofit, nonpartisan grassroots organization focused on national policies to address climate change. It trains and supports volunteers to build relationships with elected officials, the media, and their local community to work toward the adoption of fair, effective, and sustainable climate change solutions.

Climate Action Network International (CAN)

Khaldeh, Dakdouk Building, 3rd Floor

Mount Lebanon

Lebanon

Website: www.climatenetwork.org

Facebook: @CANInternational

Instagram and Twitter: @CANIntl

CAN is a worldwide network of more than 1,300 nongovernmental organizations in more than 120 countries. These groups work to promote government and individual action to limit human-induced climate change to ecologically sustainable levels.

The Climate Reality Project

750 9th Street NW, Suite 520

Washington, DC 20001

(202) 628-1999

Website: www.climaterealityproject.org

Facebook, Instagram, and Twitter: @climatereality

YouTube: Climate Reality

Climate Reality Project works to make urgent action a necessity across every level of society. Urgent actions include cutting greenhouse gas emissions, speeding the global shift to renewable energy, reducing the use of fossil fuels, and urging world leaders to strengthen and honor their Paris Agreement commitments concerning carbon emissions.

Friends of the Earth Canada

200 - 251 Bank Street

Ottawa, ON K2P 1X3

Canada

(888) 385-4444

Website: https://foecanada.org/en

Facebook: @foe.canada

Twitter: @FoE_canada

YouTube: Friends of the Earth Canada

Email: foe@foecanada.org

Friends of the Earth Canada, affiliated with Friends of the Earth International, speaks out on environmental issues, takes action to confront polluters, and holds governments responsible for their promises while insisting they enforce laws. It also provides information on environmental issues.

The Intergovernmental Panel on Climate Change (IPCC)

c/o World Meteorological Organization

7 bis Avenue de la Paix

C.P. 2300

CH- 1211 Geneva 2

Switzerland

Website: https://www.ipcc.ch

Facebook, Instagram, and Vimeo: @IPCC

Twitter: @IPCC_CH

YouTube: Intergovernmental Panel on Climate Change (IPCC)

The IPCC is the United Nations organization responsible for assessing the science related to climate change. It also issued the special report in 2018, "Global Warming of 1.5°C."

Natural Resources Defense Council (NRDC)

40 West 20th Street, 11th Floor

New York, NY 10011

(212) 727-2700

Website: www.nrdc.org

Facebook: @nrdc.org

Instagram: @nrdc_org

Twitter: @NRDC

YouTube: NRDCflix

Email: nrdcinfo@nrdc.org

The NRDC partners with businesses, political leaders, scientists, lawyers, and policy advocates across the globe to combat pollution and other threats to the planet. Its newest campaign is to prevent catastrophic climate change by transforming the way people produce electricity, make the things they need, and move people and goods around.

US Environmental Protection Agency (EPA)

1200 Pennsylvania Avenue NW

Washington, DC 20460

(202) 564-4700

Website: www.epa.gov

Facebook: @EPA

Instagram: @epagov

Twitter: @EPA

YouTube: U.S. Environmental Protection Agency

The EPA's mission is to protect human health and the environment. As part of this mission, it is creating adaptation plans for dealing with climate change and its effects on humans and the environment. It also provides information on green energy and reducing the causes of climate change.

For Further Reading

Alter, Robin. *The Anxiety Workbook for Kids: Take Charge of Fears and Worries Using the Gift of Imagination*. Oakland, CA: Instant Help, 2016.

Basher, Simon. *Basher Science: Climate Change*. New York, NY: Kingfisher Books, 2015.

Berners-Lee, Mike. *There Is No Planet B: A Handbook for the Make or Break Years*. New York, NY: Cambridge University Press, 2019.

Cunningham, Anne C., and Kenneth Philip Green. *Climate Change: A Threat to All Life on Earth* (The End of Life As We Know It). New York, NY: Enslow, 2016.

Espejo, Roman. *Can Glacier and Icemelt Be Reversed?* (At Issue). New York, NY: Greenhaven Press, 2014.

Heos, Bridget. *It's Getting Hot in Here: The Past, Present, and Future of Climate Change*. New York, NY: Houghton Mifflin Harcourt, 2016.

Herman, Gail. *What Is Climate Change?* New York, NY: Penguin Books, 2018.

Kolbert, Elizabeth. *Field Notes from a Catastrophe: Man, Nature, and Climate Change*. New York, NY: Bloomsbury USA, 2015.

Mann, Michael E., and Lee R. Kump. *Dire Predictions: The Visual Guide to the Findings of the IPCC*, 2nd Edition. New York, NY: DK Publishing, 2015.

Micco, Jamie A. *The Worry Workbook for Teens: Effective CBT Strategies to Break the Cycle of Chronic Worry and Anxiety*. Oakland, CA: Instant Help, 2017.

Mulder, Michelle. *Trash Talk: Moving Toward a Zero-Waste World*. Custer, WA: Orca Books, 2015.

Room, Joseph. *Climate Change: What Everyone Needs to Know*. New York, NY: Oxford University Press, 2018.

Santos, Rita, ed. *Geoengineering: Counteracting Climate Change* (Global Viewpoints). New York, NY: Greenhaven Press, 2018.

Bibliography

A Student's Guide to Global Climate Change. "Greenhouse Gases." Environmental Protection Agency, Retrieved January 22, 2019. https://www3.epa.gov/climatechange//kids /basics/today/greenhouse-gases.html.

American Psychological Association. "Mental Health and Our Changing Climate: Impacts, Implications, and Guidance." March 2017. https://www.apa.org/news /press/releases/2017/03/mental-health-climate.pdf.

Bennett, Jeffrey. *A Global Warming Primer: Answering Your Questions About the Science, the Consequences, and the Solutions.* Boulder, CO: Big Kid Science, 2016.

Carbon Pricing Leadership Coalition. "What Is Carbon Pricing?" Retrieved February 13, 2019. https://www .carbonpricingleadership.org/what.

Castelloe, Molly S. "Coming to Terms with Ecoanxiety." *Psychology Today*, January 9, 2018. https://www .psychologytoday.com/us/blog/the-me-in-we/201801 /coming-terms-ecoanxiety.

Davenport, Leslie. *Emotional Resiliency in the Era of Climate Change.* Philadelphia, PA: Jessica Kingsley Publishers, 2017.

Denchak, Melissa. "Paris Climate Agreement: Everything You Need to Know." NRDC, December 12, 2017. https://www.nrdc.org/stories/paris-climate-agreement -everything-you-need-know.

Edwards, Sarah Anne, and Linda Buzzell. "The Waking Up Syndrome." Good Therapy. Retrieved January 25, 2019. https://www.goodtherapy.org/blog/psychpedia/eco -anxiety.

Fearn, Rebecca. "What Is Eco-Anxiety? Here's What to Do If You're Struggling to Cope with Climate Change Warnings." Bustle, October 27, 2018. https://www .bustle.com/p/what-is-eco-anxiety-heres-what-to

-do-if-youre-struggling-to-cope-with-climate-change
-warnings-12963121.

Holthaus, Eric. "Got Those Climate Change Blues." Sierra Club, February 28, 2018. https://www.sierraclub.org /sierra/2018-2-march-april/last-words/eric-holthaus -got-those-climate-change-blues.

Intergovernmental Panel on Climate Change. "Global Warming of 1.5ºC." Retrieved January 22, 2019. https:// www.ipcc.ch/sr15.

Kaplan, E. Ann. *Climate Trauma: Foreseeing the Future in Dystopian Film and Fiction*. New Brunswick, NJ: Rutgers University Press, 2016.

Mortillaro, Nicole. "The Psychology of Climate Change: Why People Deny the Evidence." CBC Radio-Canada, December 2, 2018. https://www.cbc.ca/news/technology /climate-change-psychology-1.4920872.

National Climate Assessment. "Volume II: Impacts, Risks, and Adaptation in the United States: Summary Findings." US Global Change Assessment Program, November 2018. https://nca2018.globalchange.gov.

Plumer, Brad, and Nadja Popovich. "Why Half a Degree of Global Warming Is a Big Deal." *New York Times*, October 7, 2018. https://www.nytimes.com/interactive/2018/10/07 /climate/ipcc-report-half-degree.html.

Pritchard, Emma-Louise. "Ecoanxiety: What Is It and How Can We Treat It?" *Country Living*, November 18, 2018. https:// www.countryliving.com/uk/wellbeing/a24395537 /ecoanxiety-definition-treatment.

Schreiber, Katherine, and Heather Hausenblas. "How Climate Change Affects Mental Health." *Psychology Today*, April 1, 2017. https://www.psychologytoday.com.

Science Daily. "Intergovernmental Panel on Climate

Change." October 8, 2018. https://www.sciencedaily.com/releases/2018/10/181008075147.htm.

Stierwalt, Sabrina. "Are Extreme Weather Events Linked to Climate Change?" *Scientific American*, October 20, 2018. https://www.scientificamerican.com.

Swell Investing. "Nearly Three in Four Millennials Experience 'Ecoanxiety.'" PR Newswire, April 17, 2018. https://www.prnewswire.com/news-releases/nearly-three-in-four-millennials-experience-ecoanxiety-300630657.html

Transition United States. "The Transition Town Movement." Retrieved February 13, 2019. http://transitionus.org/transition-town-movement.

United Nations Climate Change. "The Paris Agreement." Retrieved January 21, 2019. https://unfccc.int/process-and-meetings/the-paris-agreement/the-paris-agreement.

Watson, Stephanie. "How Eco-anxiety Works." How Stuff Works. Retrieved January 20, 2019. https://science.howstuffworks.com/environmental/green-science/eco-anxiety2.htm.

Watts, Jonathan. "We Have 12 Years to Limit Climate Change Catastrophe, Warns UN." *Guardian*, October 8, 2018. https://www.theguardian.com/environment/2018/oct/08/global-warming-must-not-exceed-15c-warns-landmark-un-report.

Index

About the Author

Marcia Amidon Lusted is a writer and editor who has written numerous books and articles for young readers. She also works in sustainable development, helping communities and regions all over the world create more sustainable futures. You can learn more about Marcia Amidon Lusted's books at www .adventuresinnonfiction.com and her sustainability work at www.rubiconseven.com.

Photo Credits

Cover Chaninny/Shutterstock.com, Patricia Hamilton/Moment/Getty Images (background); p. 5 Allison Joyce/Getty Images; p. 8 Spencer Platt/Getty Images; p. 10 Library of Congress Prints and Photographs Division; p. 12 stockphoto-graf/Shutterstock.com; p. 17 Sergei Bachlakov/ Shutterstock.com; p. 19 tommaso79/Shutterstock.com; p. 23 Bernhard Staehli/Shutterstock.com; p. 25 Michael Sewell/photolibrary/Getty Images; p. 28 trgrowth/Shutterstock.com; p. 31 Monty Rakusen/Cultura/ Getty Images; p. 34 WENN Rights Ltd/Alamy Stock Photo; p. 37 Pacific Press/LightRocket/Getty Images; p. 40 David McNew/Getty Images; p. 44 Jake Lyell/Alamy Stock Photo; pp. 48-49, 87, 94 NurPhoto/Getty Images; p. 50 Barcroft/Barcroft Media/Getty Images; p. 54 Hill Street Studios/Digital Vision/Getty Images; p. 56 izusek/E+/Getty Images; p. 61 Emmanuel Dunand/AFP/Getty Images; p. 64 AlessandroBiascioli/ Shutterstock.com; p. 67 SolStock/E+/Getty Images; pp. 68–69 Syda Productions/Shutterstock.com; p. 72 piola666/E+/Getty Images; p. 77 U.S. Army photo by Sgt. 1st Class Raymond Drumsta, Joint Force Headquarters, New York Army National Guard; p. 82–83 Mario Tama/ Getty Images; p. 84 Pat Tuson/Alamy Stock Photo; p. 91 CasarsaGuru/ E+/Getty Images.

Design: Michael Moy; Layout and Photo Researcher: Ellina Litmanovich; Editor: Erin Staley